real Ninja

Over 20 true stories of Japan's secret assassins

Illustrations by JAMES FIELD

Text by STEPHEN TURNBULL

ENCHANTED LION BOOKS
New York

For Phoebe Lou, from Grandad

First American Edition published in 2008 by
Enchanted Lion Books, 201 Richards Street, Studio 4, Brooklyn, NY 11231

Conceived and produced by Breslich & Foss Ltd.
Illustrations by James Field
Text by Stephen Turnbull

Printed and bound in China

A CIP record is available from the Library of Congress

ISBN-10: 1-59270-081-0
ISBN-13: 978-1-59270-081-3

Contents

Introduction

The use in warfare of spies, assassins, and undercover elite forces has been known in every country throughout world history, and Japan is no exception. The name for Japan's "special forces" is ninja, a word that literally means "invisible men." Tracing their descent from the elite warriors of ancient China, the ninja infiltrated enemy armies to cause confusion, set fire to enemy castles, and carry out assassinations on enemy commanders, reaching their peak in the sixteenth century, the time of Japan's great civil wars.

Expert ninja

Over the years certain samurai families in Japan developed a traditional expertise in *ninjutsu*, the art of the ninja. They sold their services to the highest bidder, and could sometimes find themselves working for two rival families in turn. But many powerful *daimyo* (warlords) came to distrust them and, in 1581, the leading group of ninja families in Japan were attacked by a massive army. The surviving ninja scattered and some were taken into the service of other *daimyo* because of their military skills. Eventually they

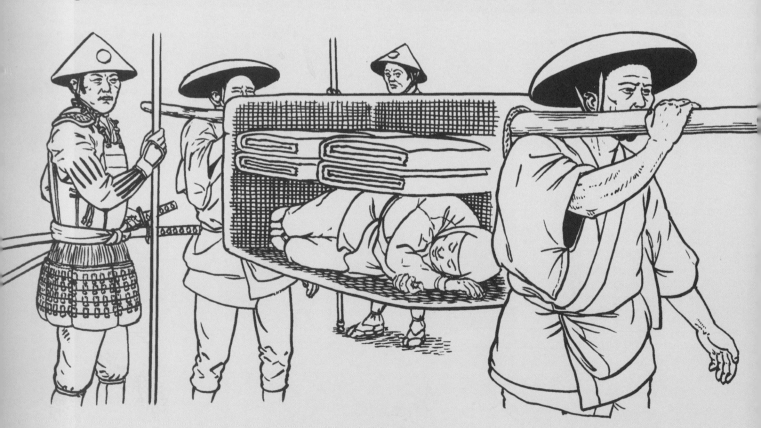

became palace guards to the *Shogun*, Japan's ruler, because of their superb military skills. Even women practiced ninja skills, learning how to climb walls or conceal themselves from prying eyes.

Spies and secret agents

The first recorded instance of the use of undercover agents in Japanese warfare occurred in the year 940, when Taira Masakado led a rebellion against the emperor. He employed a spy against his rivals, but the man was caught and put to death because the *samurai* (military officer class) despised the idea that warfare could be underhand or even undercover.

Some very clever acts of deception were, however, carried out by *samurai*, even though they always claimed to have nothing to do with ninja-like activities. Taira Tadamori, for example, was warned that someone was planning to assassinate him at the imperial court. As he sat there, Tadamori produced a dagger from inside his jacket, just to make the murderer realise that his plot had been discovered. Tadamori remained safe from assassination, but since it was against the law to carry weapons in court, he was brought before the emperor. When Tadamori showed the guards that his dagger was only made of wood, he was released and admired for his cleverness.

From samurai to ninja

Great rivalry existed between the various *samurai* clans, which came to a head with the Gempei War of 1160–1185, when the Taira and the Minamoto families fought each other. The Minamoto family won, and Minamoto Yoritomo became Japan's first *Shogun*, or military dictator, who began to rule the country in place of the emperor.

Much of Yoritomo's military success was due to his younger brother Minamoto Yoshitsune. Jealous of Yoshitsune, Yoritomo planned to kill him. Yoshitsune was forced to flee for his life when Yoritomo tried to arrest him. On his travels through Japan, Yoshitsune lived as a ninja, hiding from Yoritomo's *samurai* and disguising himself in order to pass unseen through guarded checkpoints. At one such barrier Yoshitsune and his companions had appeared disguised as *yamabushi*, the wandering mountain priests. When one of the guards seemed to recognize Yoshitsune, his companions had to think fast. His servant Benkei, who was a monk himself, took his wooden staff and hit Yoshitsune on the shoulder, shouting at him to hurry up. As no servant would ever strike his master, the guards were satisfied and let the party pass. Once they were safely through, Benkei begged his master for forgiveness.

Yoshitsune and Benkei were eventually defeated in battle, but legend credits Yoshitsune with escaping and becoming a ninja leader. Some stories suggest he sought refuge in Mongolia, where he became the great conqueror Genghis Khan!

A master of deception

The *Shoguns* ruled Japan for the next 800 years with the emperor confined to ceremonial duties. In 1331, however, Emperor Go Daigo led a revolt against the *Shogun's* rule, helped by the *samurai* Kusunoki Masashige, whose cleverness earned him the reputation of being a ninja. One day, besiegers placed ladders up against the emperor's castle wall. But the wall was only a screen of planks tied to the real wall behind. As soon as the ladders were filled with *samurai*, Masashige ordered the ropes holding the false wall to be cut. Hundreds fell to their deaths and many were injured when huge logs were rolled down the hill toward them.

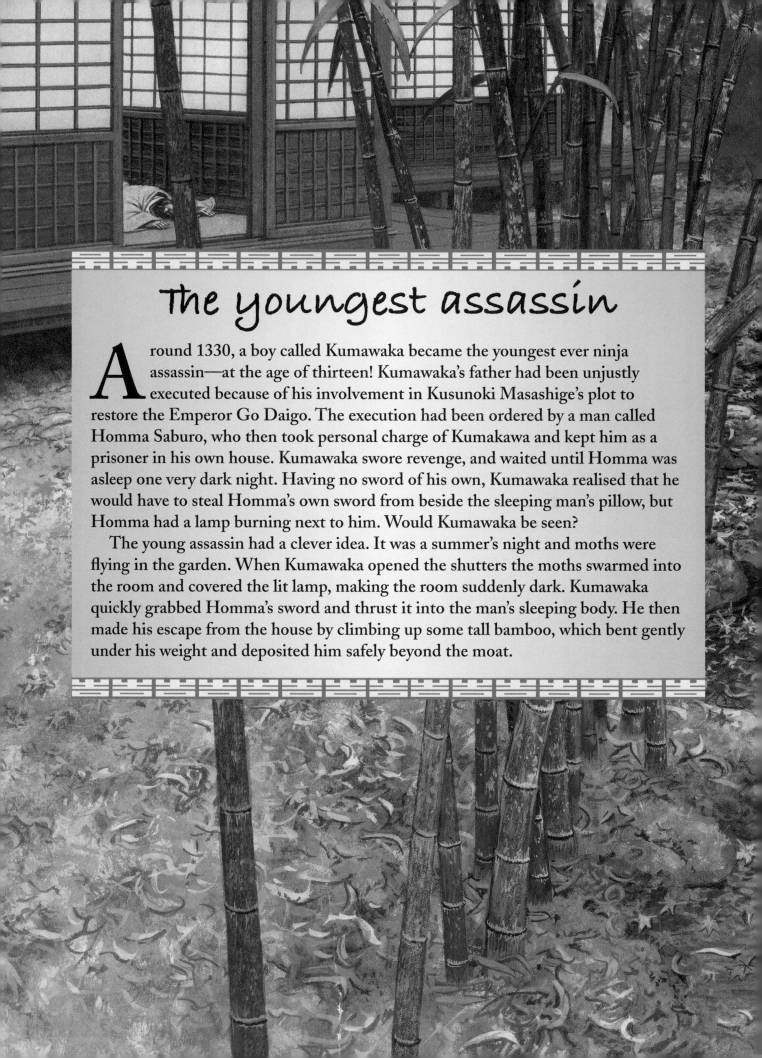

The youngest assassin

Around 1330, a boy called Kumawaka became the youngest ever ninja assassin—at the age of thirteen! Kumawaka's father had been unjustly executed because of his involvement in Kusunoki Masashige's plot to restore the Emperor Go Daigo. The execution had been ordered by a man called Homma Saburo, who then took personal charge of Kumakawa and kept him as a prisoner in his own house. Kumawaka swore revenge, and waited until Homma was asleep one very dark night. Having no sword of his own, Kumawaka realised that he would have to steal Homma's own sword from beside the sleeping man's pillow, but Homma had a lamp burning next to him. Would Kumawaka be seen?

The young assassin had a clever idea. It was a summer's night and moths were flying in the garden. When Kumawaka opened the shutters the moths swarmed into the room and covered the lit lamp, making the room suddenly dark. Kumawaka quickly grabbed Homma's sword and thrust it into the man's sleeping body. He then made his escape from the house by climbing up some tall bamboo, which bent gently under his weight and deposited him safely beyond the moat.

Men in black?

The most recognizable part of a ninja's costume was the dark-colored jacket and trousers that he wore. The jacket was tucked into the trousers to aid ease of movement. The color is usually thought to have been black, but dark blue gave better protection on a bright moonlit night. Brown or gray costumes would also be worn depending on the phases of the moon. The ninja's face was concealed by a hood and a cloth that wound around his mouth to show only his eyes. This had the advantage of hiding the sound of any heavy breathing that might disclose his presence.

Throwing weapons

Caltrops were small sharp devices that the ninja threw behind him to hinder pursuers. They were made so that no matter how they fell one spike would always face upward. Japanese *samurai* wore straw sandals on their feet, so treading on a caltrop was very painful. If a ninja could not obtain metal caltrops, he would use the seed of the water-plantain, which has very sharp spikes arranged in a triangular shape.

Concealed within the hidden pockets in the ninja's jacket were a number of different types of dart that he could throw at an enemy. Some were like big needles, others were shaped like stars and could be flicked, spinning very quickly in flight. All were so sharp that they cut deeply, even into wooden planks.

The ninja sword

The ninja sword was like an ordinary *samurai* sword, but fitted with an extra large sword guard that could provide a foothold if a ninja had need of one to help him climb over a wall. He did this by placing the sword against

the wall and his foot into the loop of cord that ran from the handle. When he was on top of the wall, he would lift his leg and the sword followed.

Clever disguises

Civil wars continued in Japan for years as *samurai* families fought each other for supremacy. Their armies were all similar in size and weapons, so how was one *daimyo* to gain an advantage over another? One way was to use ninja to spy and carry out assassinations or surprise attacks. This led to an increasing demand for undercover warfare and, as the years went by, certain families began to specialize in *ninjutsu*, selling their services to anyone who would employ them. The most important center for ninja lay deep in the mountains of central Japan in the areas known as Iga and Koga. This was a land of secret wooded valleys protected by narrow mountain passes. It was easy to defend, and an excellent base for developing skills in ninja warfare. The skills of *ninjutsu* were passed from father to son and, from the fifteenth century onward, the ninja from Iga and Koga were hired by local *daimyo* in their wars with rivals.

Rival *daimyo* would sometimes hire different groups of Iga ninja, although the ninja were very careful not to fight each other. In 1558 Rokkaku Yoshikata employed Iga ninja to capture a castle. They disguised themselves to look like the castle guards, even making paper lanterns with the commander's badge on them. They were so convincing that the castle gates were readily opened to them! The ninja then showed their true colors by setting fire to the castle.

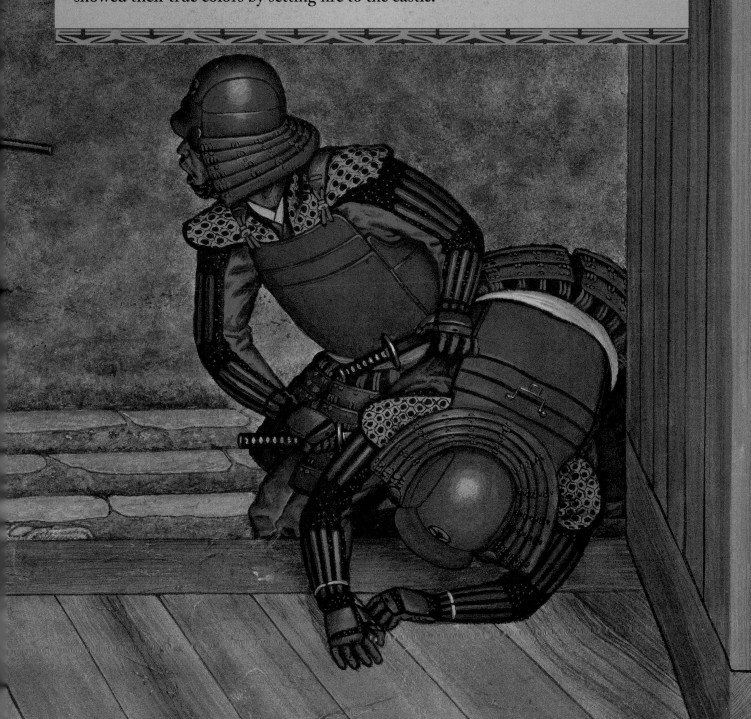

Training a young ninja

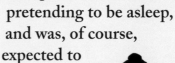

A boy, or occasionally a girl, born into a ninja family in Iga or Koga undertook specialized training from a very early age. The military skills of archery and swordsmanship that were needed by any *samurai* family were included, but the ninja trainee went much further in his expertise. For example, in addition to superb swordplay, a young boy was expected to become proficient in the use of darts and other throwing weapons, and to be able to defend himself with his bare hands if necessary. Youngsters, trained to be physically fit, learned to climb walls, swim under water for long distances, and survive outdoors for long periods.

Specialized ninja techniques, kept as closely guarded secrets by ninja families, included blending poisons, picking locks, and using gunpowder bombs. A ninja was also trained in how to recognize if a potential victim was only pretending to be asleep, and was, of course, expected to kill without mercy whenever it was required.

A successful ambush

A *daimyo* called Oda Nobunaga was very concerned about the influence of the Iga ninja's secret operations. By the year 1580, Oda Nobunaga looked as though he would control the whole of Japan one day, so he sent his son on an expedition into Iga to control the ninja families. It was a disastrous failure. The Oda army was ambushed as it crossed the mountain pass and many *samurai* were killed. In 1581 Oda Nobunaga led a much bigger expedition in person. He coordinated five armies to invade Iga from five directions at once. The ninja families did not know from where the main attack would come, and their bases fell in spite of fierce resistance. Yet none could have anticipated what was to happen the following year. On his way to lead another military expedition, Oda Nobunaga was ambushed by one of his own generals and died in the fighting. It was a victory of which any ninja would have been proud!

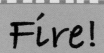

Fire!

In 1541 the area just to the north of the ninja homelands was in turmoil. An ambitious *daimyo* called Miyoshi Chokei invaded the lands of a neighbor called Kizawa Nagamasa. Nagamasa's main base was Kasagi castle, the same place that had fallen to a ninja attack 200 years earlier (page 8). Miyoshi Chokei was taking no chances, so he hired a group of ninja from Iga to lead his operation. Their mission was to set fire to Kasagi castle before Miyoshi's *samurai* moved in, a task they accomplished very cleverly. Mount Kasagi, on which the castle was built, also had a Buddhist temple in the woods on its peak. Unusual though it was for ninja to attack monks, once they realized the temple was likely to be lightly guarded, they climbed up and set fire to it, and the flames soon spread to the castle. Kizawa Nagamasa had no alternative but to order his guards out of the castle to try and put the fires out. As soon as the guards were engaged in their task, Miyoshi Chokei's *samurai* launched a furious attack on the castle.

A quick-thinking general

After assassinating Oda Nobunaga (page 17), his murderer, a *samurai* general called Akechi Mitsuhide, hurried to take over Nobunaga's territories. One of his most dangerous opponents was the *daimyo* Tokugawa Ieyasu, who decided to hurry back to his own province to raise an army. The quickest way back was through Iga, where Ieyasu had powerful friends among the surviving ninja families who would act as guides.

At one river crossing, Ieyasu's ninja friends concealed him under the bales of rice that covered the deck. Just before the boat set off, a number of Akechi Mitsuhide's *samurai* arrived and began to search the vessel. They could not move the tightly pcacked rice bales so they thrust their spears through them to see if anyone was hiding there. One of the spears cut Ieyasu's leg, but he thought quickly and wiped the blade clean of blood as it was being withdrawn so that no one would know he was hiding there!

The Iga ninjas' generosity in helping in this escape was never forgotten. When Tokugawa Ieyasu became *Shogun* in the year 1600, Iga and Koga ninja became hereditary palace guards for the Tokugawa family.

Paying your ninja

The ninja from Iga and Koga did not work on their own. They belonged to groups of ninja families whose leader was also the village headman. He undertook negotiations with *daimyo* who wanted to hire ninja services. Individual ninja would then be selected for the mission. Payment for ninja services was made in secrecy so as not to compromise any future arrangements. Unlike *samurai*, who were given grants to rice lands, ninja were paid in cash, usually copper or silver coins. The fee was paid to the group leader.

Weapons and equipment

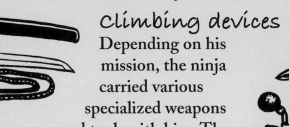

Climbing devices

Depending on his mission, the ninja carried various specialized weapons and tools with him. The most important of these would help him climb into a castle or a defended building: a rope with a hook on the end enabled him to get to the top of a wall; metal hooks with large handles allowed him to get a grip inside the crevices of stone walls; wide metal clamps could be hammered into the wall to make a foothold.

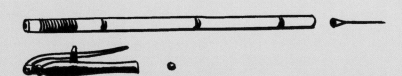

Rockets and guns

The ninja used a wide array of gunpowder devices. When ninja acted as snipers, they used matchlock muskets, but if a ninja was planning to enter a castle, bombs and rockets were more useful.

Smoke bombs could provide a smoke screen for the ninja to escape; small firecrackers on a string would make enemies believe that a large number of ninja was attacking; fire rockets allowed a ninja to set fire to a castle tower from far away, and bombs filled with pieces of iron were used to kill the enemy guards.

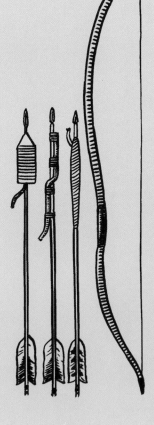

Burglars' tools

The ninja were expert burglars! They could pick locks using delicate iron spikes. They broke through castle walls by twisting a wide iron blade into the plaster covering to crumble it away and then sawed through the wooden framework beneath the plaster. They used iron levers to force open wooden shutters and doors, or cut through them with very sharp saw blades.

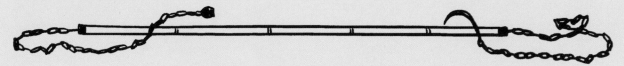

Sickle and chain

The ninja would use all the weapons that were associated with *samurai* such as swords, spears and bows, but were also expert at wielding strange weapons derived from agricultural tools. For example, a sickle normally used by farmers to harvest the rice crop would have its blade sharpened, making it ideal as a slashing weapon. To the base of the wooden handle a long iron chain was fixed with a weight on the end. The ninja would whirl the chain around his head very quickly and then throw it at a *samurai* to wrap the chain around his sharp sword blade. The ninja could then drag the sword out of the man's hands and finish him off with the sickle blade.

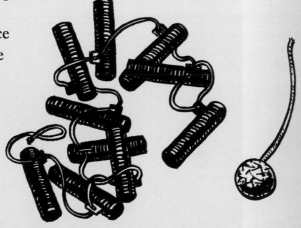

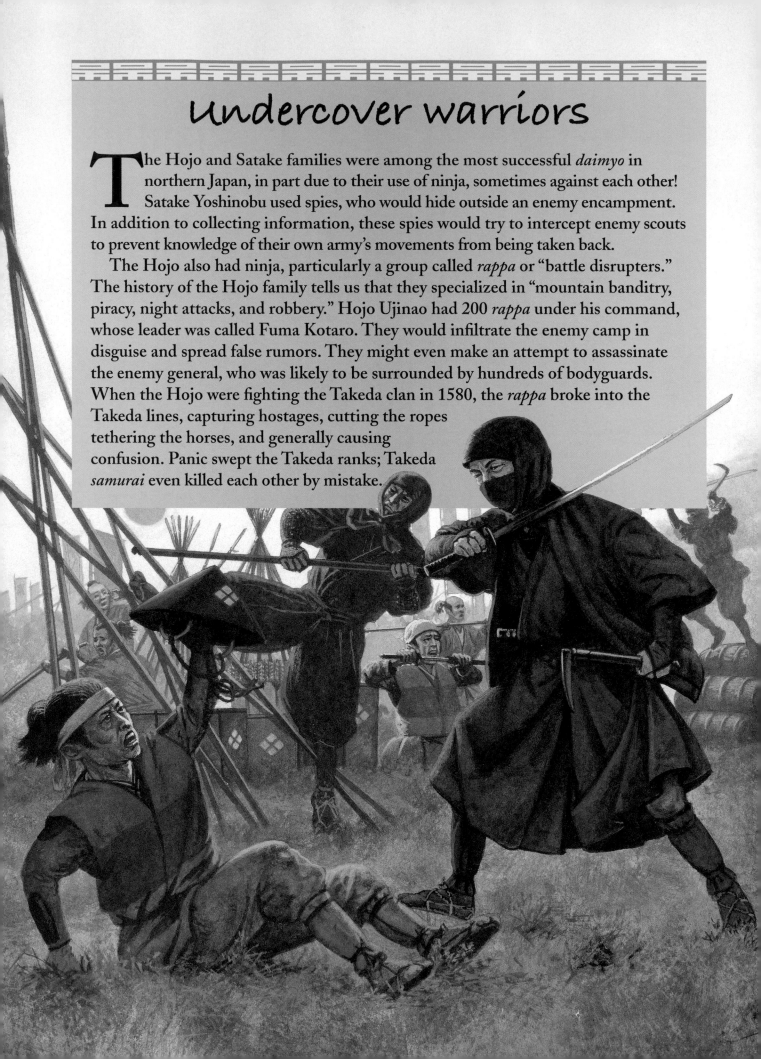

Undercover warriors

The Hojo and Satake families were among the most successful *daimyo* in northern Japan, in part due to their use of ninja, sometimes against each other! Satake Yoshinobu used spies, who would hide outside an enemy encampment. In addition to collecting information, these spies would try to intercept enemy scouts to prevent knowledge of their own army's movements from being taken back.

The Hojo also had ninja, particularly a group called *rappa* or "battle disrupters." The history of the Hojo family tells us that they specialized in "mountain banditry, piracy, night attacks, and robbery." Hojo Ujinao had 200 *rappa* under his command, whose leader was called Fuma Kotaro. They would infiltrate the enemy camp in disguise and spread false rumors. They might even make an attempt to assassinate the enemy general, who was likely to be surrounded by hundreds of bodyguards. When the Hojo were fighting the Takeda clan in 1580, the *rappa* broke into the Takeda lines, capturing hostages, cutting the ropes tethering the horses, and generally causing confusion. Panic swept the Takeda ranks; Takeda *samurai* even killed each other by mistake.

Kidnapped!

One of the most successful ninja operations was commissioned by Tokugawa Ieyasu (page 20). When he was young he was in the service of a powerful *daimyo* called Imagawa Yoshimoto, whose huge army was unexpectedly defeated in 1560. When Yoshimoto was killed, his son Ujizane took the families of the leading *samurai* hostage, including Tokugawa Ieyasu's family, to guarantee their continued loyalty and good behavior.

Tokugawa Ieyasu realized that the only way to break free of the Imagawa clan would be to take hostages of his own and exchange them for his relatives. A raiding party of Koga ninja sneaked into one of Ujizane's castles so secretly that when the Udono family, who held the castle, discovered that some of their fortress towers were on fire and their guards were being killed, they thought their own men had turned traitor!

Two hundred Udono *samurai* were burned to death in the attack, but this was much less important for Tokugawa Ieyasu than the capture of Udono's two sons. They were speedily traded for Ieyasu's own family, freeing him from Imagawa domination. The Udono sons were later returned to their castle by Imagawa. Not long afterward they started a campaign against Tokugawa Ieyasu, who was forced to send ninja to attack them. It proved to be another successful raid, making the Udono brothers the only leaders in *samurai* history to be defeated by the same ninja twice!

Ninja at Sekigahara

The decisive victory through which Tokugawa Ieyasu became *Shogun* was the huge battle of Sekigahara in 1600. Prior to the battle, the castle of Fushimi, a vital part of Ieyasu's defence, fell to enemy forces. Koga ninja took part in a stubborn if unsuccessful defence, slipping out from the castle to harass the besiegers. When the castle finally fell, one hundred of them had been killed.

The battle of Sekigahara itself was fought in the fog and drizzle of a cold October morning, and is notable for a unique use of ninja as the battle came to an end. The Shimazu family, who were on the defeated side, had trained a corps of ninja sharpshooters, who covered the Shimazu retreat by lying in wait for pursuers. Suddenly, galloping out of the mist, there appeared the distinctive bright red armor of Ii Naomasa, one of Tokugawa Ieyasu's leading generals. Taking careful aim, one of the snipers fired his musket and shattered Naomasa's elbow.

The siege of Osaka castle

The victory at Sekigahara allowed Tokugawa Ieyasu to become *Shogun*, but he still had enemies to contend with. In 1614, thousands of discontented *samurai* packed themselves into Osaka, Japan's largest castle. A huge siege by the Tokugawa army began, and once again ninja were involved. They climbed up the walls using their special tools and caused disruption among the defenders.

Ii Naomasa had died from the wounds he received at Sekigahara, so his magnificent red-armored *samurai* were now led by his son Naotaka. He had ninja in his service who acted as spies and may have been involved in negotiating a truce. During the truce period, part of the castle was destroyed and in 1615 it finally fell to the Tokugawa who burned it to the ground.

starving samurai

Ninja were involved in the last *samurai* battle: the siege of Shimabara in 1638. It followed a rebellion against the harsh rule of the *daimyo* Matsukura, who controlled the Shimabara peninsula on behalf of the Tokugawa family. The rebellion was led by a fanatical *samurai*, Amakusa Shiro, a Christian. Christianity was banned in Japan, so this gave the *Shogun* reason to ensure the rebellion was crushed. But the rebels held firm. Barricading themselves inside an old castle called Hara, they defied the *Shogun*'s *samurai* for over a year.

Desperate measures were called for and ninja also played a major role. Ninja raids were launched to capture or destroy the castle's precious rice supplies. They climbed the walls, then kicked over the pine torches that provided illumination. The resulting flames caused much damage. Toward the end of the siege, the Tokugawa mounted a ninja spying raid to see how long the enemy's food supplies would last. When they discovered that the Hara *samurai* were reduced to eating seaweed, the Tokugawa attacked. Fierce resistance was mounted, but the defending *samurai* were now too weak to fight off the raiders.

29

Ninja disguises

Even though the ninja are best known for being dressed in black for night raids, they had to be masters of disguise. Enemy guards could be completely fooled if the ninja dressed exactly as they did, wearing the *daimyo*'s own badge on identical suits of armor. The ninja were able to recognize each other by using secret passwords, and could cause havoc in enemy castles.

traveling through the countryside were the numerous checkpoints set up on the borders between Japanese provinces. Baggage would be searched and travelers' identities rigorously checked. Ninja coped with this by choosing to disguise themselves as people who were regarded as outcasts from society. Entertainers and actors, who always wandered from place to place, were seldom registered, so if a ninja passed himself

Checkpoint disguises

The greatest danger for ninja

off as an actor he would probably be allowed through a checkpoint with no questions asked. One aspect of ninja training was therefore to teach them to sing and dance so that no one would suspect their real identity.

Ninja or monk?

Another good disguise was that of a wandering priest. The wild-looking *yamabushi*, who specialized in praying on the top of high mountains, were feared because of their tough appearance and their readiness to utter curses. Few *samurai* would dare try to arrest them. The strange *komuso*, wandering priests who belonged to the Zen sect, traveled around Japan playing the flute beneath huge basket hats that completely disguised their faces. As well as hiding a ninja's identity, the *komuso* disguise provided cover for a secret weapon, because the bamboo flute could easily be converted into a blow pipe for poisoned darts.

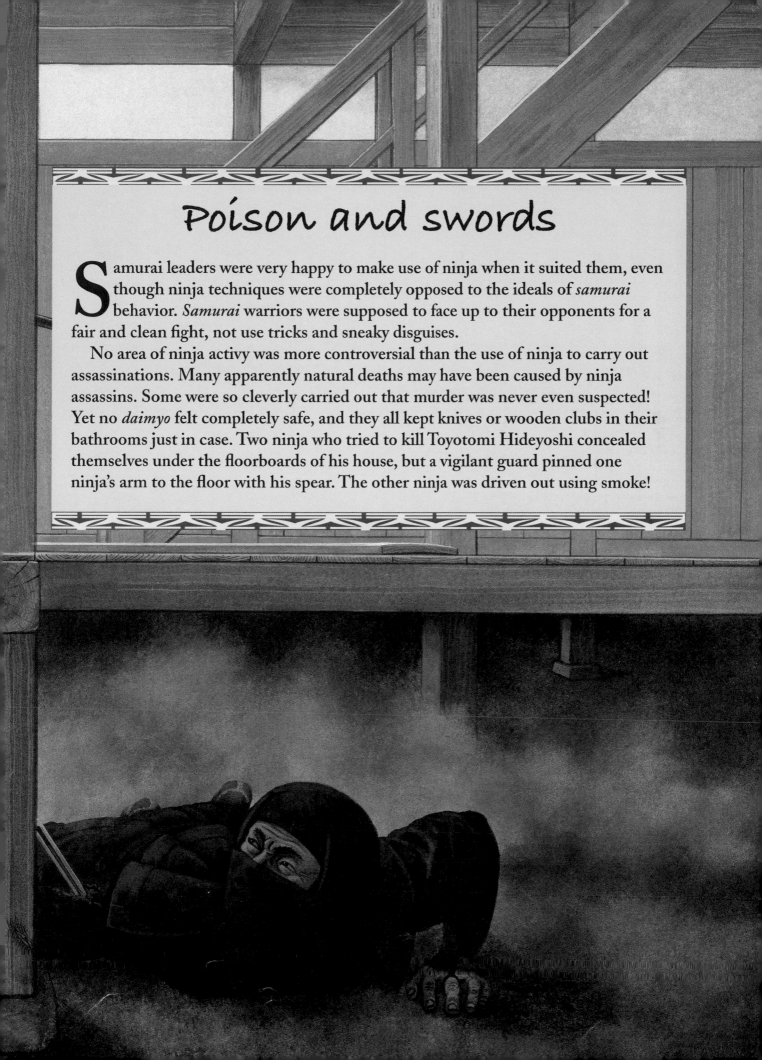

Poison and swords

Samurai leaders were very happy to make use of ninja when it suited them, even though ninja techniques were completely opposed to the ideals of *samurai* behavior. *Samurai* warriors were supposed to face up to their opponents for a fair and clean fight, not use tricks and sneaky disguises.

No area of ninja activy was more controversial than the use of ninja to carry out assassinations. Many apparently natural deaths may have been caused by ninja assassins. Some were so cleverly carried out that murder was never even suspected! Yet no *daimyo* felt completely safe, and they all kept knives or wooden clubs in their bathrooms just in case. Two ninja who tried to kill Toyotomi Hideyoshi concealed themselves under the floorboards of his house, but a vigilant guard pinned one ninja's arm to the floor with his spear. The other ninja was driven out using smoke!

Lucky escapes

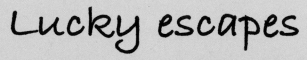

Oda Nobunaga, the man who conquered the ninja homelands in 1581 (page 17), was the target of several ninja assassination attempts during his lifetime. Rokkaku Yoshizuke, a *daimyo* who had lost a lot of territory to Nobunaga, hired a ninja to kill him in 1571. The ninja was a trained sniper and lay in wait for his victim as he was crossing a mountain pass. He fired two bullets, which both struck home, but Nobunaga was saved by his body armor.

Two years later a further attempt was made by a ninja who managed to break into Nobunaga's castle of Azuchi, but he was stopped by two guards. Another ninja gained access to the ceiling

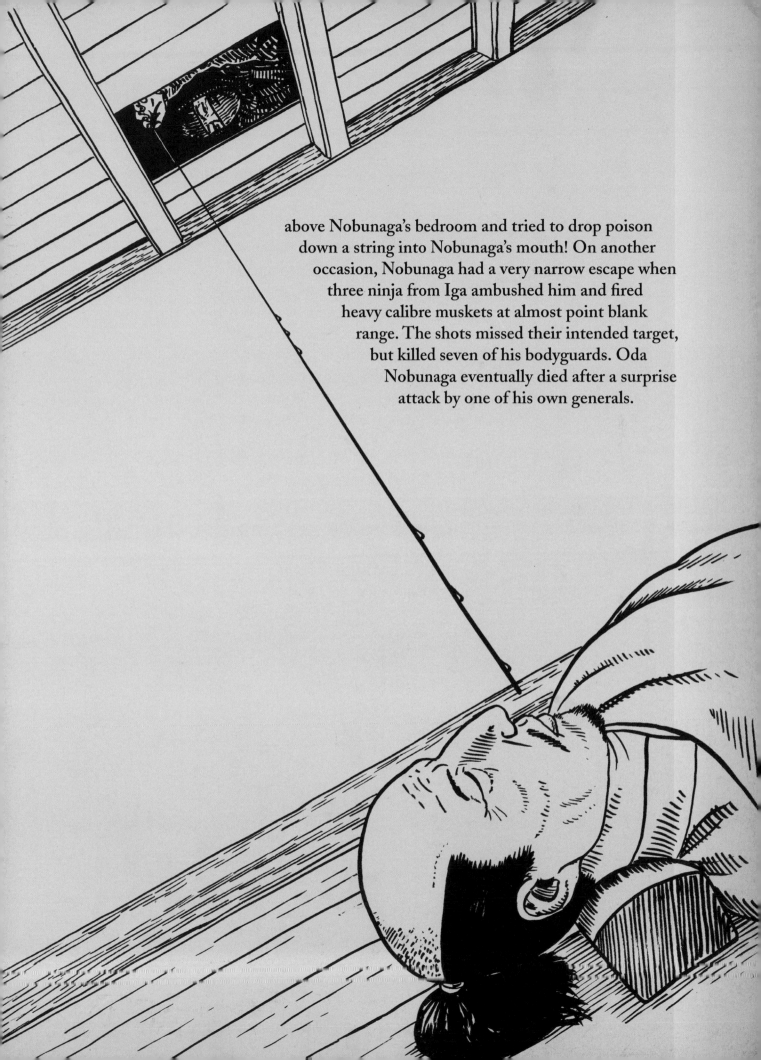

above Nobunaga's bedroom and tried to drop poison down a string into Nobunaga's mouth! On another occasion, Nobunaga had a very narrow escape when three ninja from Iga ambushed him and fired heavy calibre muskets at almost point blank range. The shots missed their intended target, but killed seven of his bodyguards. Oda Nobunaga eventually died after a surprise attack by one of his own generals.

A mysterious death

Uesugi Kenshin was one of the most powerful *daimyo* in Japan and survived several attempts on his life. He had once defeated Oda Nobunaga in battle, so Nobunaga was one of those who wanted him dead. His wish came true in 1578, but no one ever discovered if Kenshin's death was caused by a ninja assassination. For several years Kenshin had suffered from poor health and he may have had stomach cancer. One night he collapsed while in his bathroom, never regained consciousness, and died a few days later.

It was not long before strange rumors began, and it was believed that Kenshin had not died from illness but had been killed by a ninja! The story was that Kenshin's assassin had been a highly trained ninja who had sneaked into Kenshin's castle and hidden himself inside the toilet area for several days. When Kenshin was there—all alone, of course—the ninja had stabbed him to death. As Kenshin never spoke again before he died, no one knew what had really happened. As far as Oda Nobunaga was concerned, all that mattered was that his great rival was dead.

slain!

It is strange that Oda Nobunaga, who had survived attempts on his life by skilled ninja, was killed by one of his generals, but he was. Oda Nobunaga was staying in a temple in Kyoto, ready to move west to assist Toyotomi Hideyoshi who was having trouble laying siege to a castle. He sent Akechi Mitsuhide on ahead. Mitsuhide realized that Oda Nobunaga was in the temple with only the protection of his bodyguard, so he turned around and attacked. No one knows how Nobunaga died. Perhaps he committed suicide.

Breaking into a castle

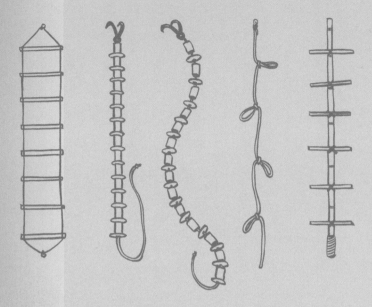

by a trained ninja who had hooks and clamps to help him. Most castles, however, were surrounded by a wide, deep moat filled with water that had to be crossed first. One way to do this was to throw a hooked rope across or fire one using a rocket and then use the rope to swing from hand-to-hand across the moat.

Water spiders

There were several other ingenious devices to allow a ninja to cross a moat. A ninja could make use of collapsible boats or an inflated ox-hide. If the moat was not deep or the ground was swampy, it might be possible to use the curious water shoes known as water spiders. These allowed the ninja to skim across a flooded area, but would not give the buoyancy necessary to float in deep water.

Japanese castles were built on very solid stone bases designed to slope outward to protect against the shock of earthquakes. The bases had gaps between the stones, so they were quite easy to climb, particularly

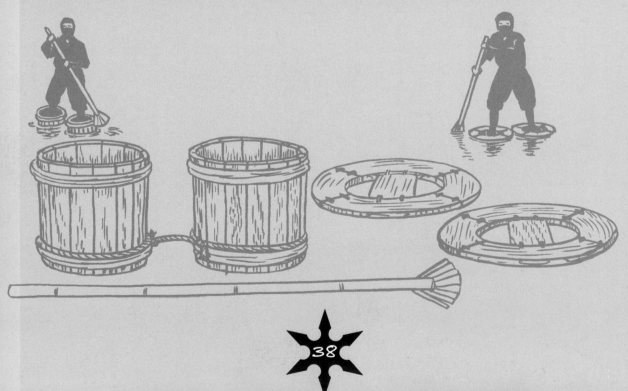

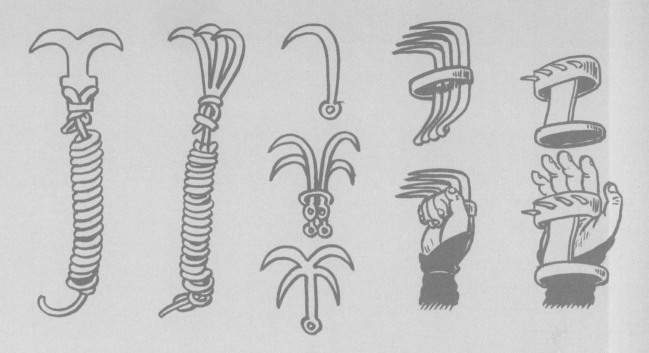

Collapsible ladders

Collapsible ladders made from bamboo helped ninja climb over the smooth plastered walls that were built on top of a castle's big stone base. Ropes passed through sections of bamboo were then pulled tight and knotted securely to produce a ladder that could bear the ninja's weight for a short time.

Climbing and jumping

If all else failed, the ninja had to rely on his own climbing and jumping abilities. Ninja were known to use a *samurai*'s long spear as a pole vault, or to make a human pyramid so that a ninja could reach the top of a castle wall by climbing on to his friends' shoulders!

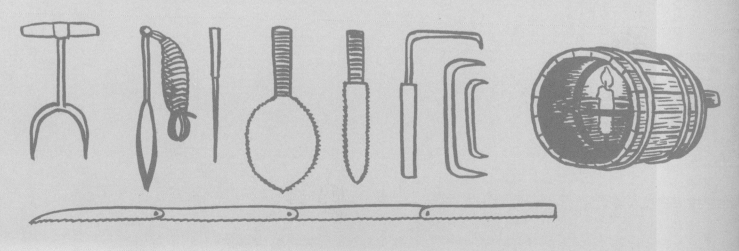

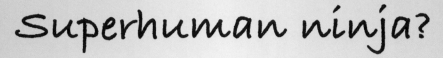

Superhuman ninja?

People thought that the ninja were superhuman because they appeared from nowhere in the middle of the night and then disappeared. *Samurai* would suddenly fall into pits that appeared in the ground filled with sharp stakes. How could men who did that be merely human? Not surprisingly, the ninja encouraged these ideas because they increased their prestige and made the *daimyo* more frightened of them! They also made the *daimyo* more willing to employ ninja to eliminate a rival. Yet the ninja warriors were supermen in only one respect: they trained more severely than any samurai, and no *samurai* could have survived outdoors for the long periods of time that a ninja could. One clever survival technique was to cook rice by wrapping it in a wet cloth and building a fire over it. The rice would be steamed without the use of a cooking pot. After eating, the ninja would lie down to sleep over the place where the fire had been, thus keeping himself warm through the night.

Ninja knowledge

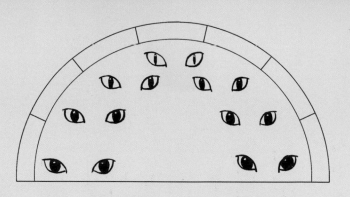

The ninja possessed secret knowledge that was denied to ordinary *samurai*. For example, ninja learned to tell the time by looking at cats' eyes, because a cat's pupils dilate with the changing of the light. Ninja also knew how to make a simple compass from a needle. They could forecast the weather by observing the moon's color and the flight of birds.

A ninja was educated from birth in the knowledge of food and medicines that could be obtained from plants. He knew how to make a shelter, and how to keep himself warm. All ninja knew how to distinguish between water that was safe to drink and water that may have been poisoned by an enemy. Massage and acupuncture kept a ninja in shape while on a mission and could help in the treatment of wounds. If a ninja was wounded in action he could apply first aid that would enable him to survive long enough to get home. Most importantly, he accepted that if he was mortally wounded he would probably have to commit suicide, so that any secrets he possessed would die with him. Ninja were as ruthless with themselves as they were with any of their victims.

invisible men

Not surprisingly, the use ninja made of their secret knowledge gave them the reputation of being men who could perform magic. Once again, this reputation pleased the ninja. They performed strange religious rituals which involved twisting their fingers while deep in meditation. Priests who were not ninja did similar things, but with ninja it was regarded as a way of becoming invisible, or of calling down a curse on an enemy. By such techniques, rumor had it, ninja could change themselves into birds and animals.

Men who fly?

Of all the myths that grew up about ninja, none was more persistent than the belief that ninja could fly. Perhaps it was because they seemed to appear from nowhere on a castle wall, having crossed a wide moat as if by magic. It was even suggested that they could have bamboo wings fitted to their shoulders and be fired from a catapult to glide into castles!

Strangely, though, one man did almost fly and this incident may be behind the idea of flying ninja. The story tells us that there were two golden dolphins on the roof of Nagoya castle, placed there as lucky charms against earthquakes and storm damage. The scales of the dolphins were covered with pure gold, and a very clever thief in Nagoya had the idea of being floated up onto the castle roof on a kite!

Apparently he almost succeeded in his daring theft. A huge kite was built, and one windy night an accomplice held the ropes while he soared up on to the roof without being spotted. But once he had chiseled off the precious gold from the dolphins and loaded it into his bag he became too heavy to glide down again. Instead, he sank slowly into the castle courtyard where he was arrested red-handed by the guards!

the ninja house

The houses where the *jonin* (leading ninja) lived were protected from attack by enemies, including other ninja! A ninja house looked like an ordinary farmhouse, but it contained several surprises. Like any Japanese house, it was built around long polished wooden corridors from which rooms were entered. Inside the rooms were simple *tatami* (straw mats) where the *jonin* received his guests. What the guests did not know was that their every word was overheard by guards who were concealed by the paper scrolls hanging on the walls.

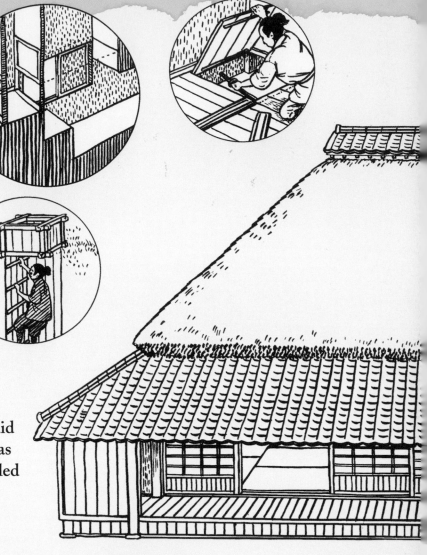

Secret passages and booby traps

If an assassination was attempted, the *jonin* could escape down the corridor, where booby traps and secret passages lay in wait for an assassin. Doors that appeared to be sliding doors in fact rotated. A ladder would drop down from the ceiling, allowing the owner to escape upstairs and then quickly pull the ladder up behind him. Floorboards would drop away to reveal poisoned iron spikes. Weapons might be hidden underneath other floorboards at places known only to the owner of the house.

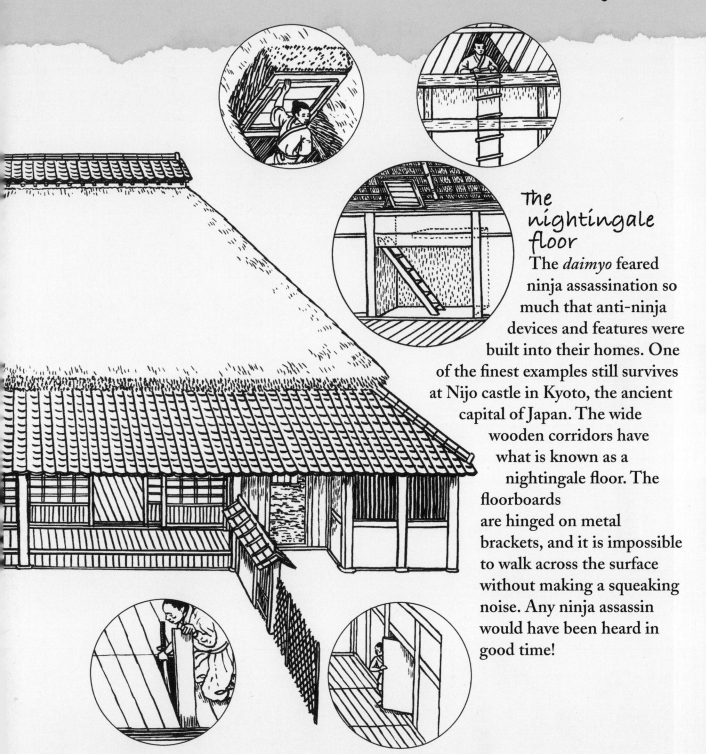

The nightingale floor

The *daimyo* feared ninja assassination so much that anti-ninja devices and features were built into their homes. One of the finest examples still survives at Nijo castle in Kyoto, the ancient capital of Japan. The wide wooden corridors have what is known as a nightingale floor. The floorboards are hinged on metal brackets, and it is impossible to walk across the surface without making a squeaking noise. Any ninja assassin would have been heard in good time!

47

Glossary

Further Reading

Louie Stowell, *Samurai* (London: Usborne Young Reading 2007)

Stephen Turnbull, *Real Samurai: Over 20 true stories about the knights of old Japan* (New York: Enchanted Lion Books, 2007)

Cheryl Aylward Whiteseale, *Blue Fingers: A Ninja's Tale* (New York: Clarion, 2004)

Stephen K. Hayes, *Ninja and their Secret Fighting Art* (Tuttle Publishing, 1990)

Masaaki Hatsumi, *The Way of the Ninja: Secret Techniques* (Kodansha International, 2004)

Websites to visit

www.ninjutsu.com/ninjakids/index.html
    Relates history, stories, ninja vocabulary, weapons and warrior creed
http://web-japan.org/kidsweb/travel/ninja/index.html
    About ninja and famous ninja villages

Index